May God's grace
abound and keep
you in peace.
Bobbie

I love you &
cherish your
friendship –
God bless you –
Sandra

$\mathcal{F}$or

Pam

$\mathcal{H}$ere's just one of the things
I love about you:

_____

_____

_____

$\mathcal{W}$ith all my love,

Bobbie & Sandra

Because
of *Love*

Celebrations of the Heart

William and Patricia Coleman

VINE
BOOKS

SERVANT PUBLICATIONS
ANN ARBOR, MICHIGAN

© 1998 by William and Patricia Coleman
All rights reserved.

Vine Books is an imprint of Servant Publications especially designed to serve evangelical Christians.

Unless otherwise noted, Scriptures have been taken from the HOLY BIBLE, NEW INTERNATIONAL VERSION®. © 1973, 1978, 1984 by International Bible Society. Used by permission of Zondervan Publishing House. All rights reserved.

The quote from Jimmy Carter is from: Gary Smith, "What Makes Jimmy Run?" *Life* (November 1995): 108.

The excerpt on page 37 is taken from: Michael Reagan and Bob Phillips, *The All-American Quote Book* (Eugene, Ore.: Harvest House, 1995). Used by permission.

The quotes from C.S. Lewis are taken from: Wayne Martindale and Jerry Root, eds., *The Quotable Lewis* (Wheaton, Ill.: Tyndale House, 1989). All rights reserved. Used by permission.

The quote from Robert Fulghum is taken from: Robert Fulghum, *All I Really Need to Know I Learned in Kindergarten* (New York: Villard, 1988), viii.

The quote from Leo Buscaglia is taken from: Leo Buscaglia, *Born for Love* (Thorofare, N.J.: Slack, 1992), 21.

The Linus quote is taken from: Michael Reagan and Bob Phillips, *The All-American Quote Book* (Eugene, Ore.: Harvest House, 1995). Used by permission.

Published by Servant Publications
P.O. Box 8617
Ann Arbor, Michigan 48107

Cover design and illustration: Paz Design Group

99 00 01 02 10 9 8 7 6 5 4 3 2 1

Printed in the United States of America
ISBN 1-56955-110-3

Library of Congress Cataloging-in-Publication Data

Coleman, William L.
Because of love : celebrations of the heart / William and Patricia Coleman.
    p.   cm.
"Vine books."
Sequel to: Because we're friends.
ISBN 1-56955-110-3 (alk. paper)
1. Love. 2. Love—Religious aspects—Christianity. I. Coleman, Patricia. II. Title
BF575.L8C64   1998
241'.4—dc21   98-31346   CIP

To Bill, from Pat
To Pat, from Bill

We have spent many years in the school of love, continually teaching each other. Thanks for the lessons, both the day classes and the night classes.

We also want to extend our thanks to Heidi Hess and the staff at Servant Publications. Their vision and hard work have made this book a reality.

God is love.

1 JOHN 4:16

Table of Contents

Love was as subtly catched, as a disease;

But being got it is a treasure sweet,

Which to defend is harder than to get:

And ought not be prophaned on either part,

For though 'tis got by chance, 'tis kept by art.

JOHN DONNE

Just Between Us

We all can walk through this world if we have love. We may have to make this journey without money or without health or without playing a guitar. Love is one thing we truly need.

Fortunately, it is also the one thing we are guaranteed. We know someone will love us. God makes that a certainty.

Because we are made in God's image, we also possess a tremendous capacity to love. The kind of love that puts a bounce in our step and a gleam in our eye. If at this moment you can think of a few people who love you like that, and whom you love like that, you can consider yourself one of the most fortunate folks on the planet.

Sometimes love gets a bad rap. That's why we wrote this book. We want to remind ourselves how good and healthy love can be. Love's return is greater than that of any other investment in life. Love is worth the work. Love is worth the dedication.

Turn the pages and let it flow. Let love roll over you like cool water from a mountain stream on a hot summer afternoon.

Bill and Pat Coleman

Part One:

True Love Is Timeless

Let us not become weary in doing good, for at the proper time we will reap a harvest if we do not give up. Therefore, as we have opportunity, let us do good to all people, especially to those who belong to the family of believers.

GALATIANS 6:9, 10

Love in the Mall

(Theologian) Reinhold Niebuhr said: The highest calling of a human being is unselfish love—to love without being loved back, without any self-interest.

JIMMY CARTER

Half awake on a crisp fall morning I drove to the local mall. My health, my girth and my doctor had all chimed in to tell me I needed to walk, even if it was inconvenient.

Pulling into the parking lot, I was surprised by the number of cars already there. "Why so many at this unspeakable hour?" I wondered.

Soon I had my answer. Inside I found a large flock of people of all sizes and all ages, walking at every variety of speed. Fathers and husbands, mothers and wives strode purposefully with a look of intense concentration. Young mothers pushed strollers and chatted as they raced along.

Rounding the first lap I noticed the number of couples that were walking together, and received my second surprise that morning. I had never before realized just how much love could be found at the mall. Love at every stage of life.

Young couples in sporty sweat suits and stylish sneakers, arms swinging steadily, passed many of the other walkers. They looked as though they were in love for the long haul, determined to stay fit to enjoy each other's company.

Couples in their fifties and sixties were there, too. Usually one partner looked overweight and out of shape. I couldn't help but wonder about these couples. What had prompted this exercise drive? Was it a passing fad ... or perhaps something more serious? A doctor's warning, perhaps, or a borderline reading on a blood test or a blood pressure check. Whatever the reason, they were here now. Together. The slimmer mate would walk alongside, not even breaking a sweat, quietly encouraging the winded partner to keep going.

The elderly couples were really special. A man and woman in their early seventies held hands as they rounded the far end of the corridor and headed for another lap. Most moving of all was one couple who appeared to be in their eighties. Slowly they plodded, side by side. Her walk was exaggerated, her gait awkward. She appeared to be recovering from hip surgery. Proud and determined, heads lifted high, this fine couple greeted the morning by taking on life's challenges one small step at a time.

I never would have imagined that such love was alive and thriving in the local mall, somewhere between the women's apparel store and the Italian fast-food restaurant. Love of all ages. Love in all conditions. Love that's glad to be alive.

I Missed You

Immature love says: "I love you because I need you."
Mature love says: "I need you because I love you."

ERICH FROMM

Whenever his son Ben has been away for an afternoon or evening, Tim welcomes him at the door. "I'm glad to see you," Dad begins, scooping up his bright-eyed preschooler. "Did you have a good time?"

To that question Ben gives an automatic, "Yes."

Then Tim puts the crown on the emotional pyramid by saying with great sincerity, "Ben, I missed you."

The strong, reassuring, honest statement connects with Ben. Often Ben will look directly into his father's eyes and reply, "I missed you too, Dad."

"I missed you" is emotional hot chocolate in the world of parenting. It's a freshly baked cookie. It's a back rub. It's a warm fuzzy. It's a feeling that we will remember long after we forget what gave us that feeling.

Another little boy was asked what he thought would make his parents the happiest. His answer: "To get a baby sitter and get rid of me."

He doesn't believe his parents ever miss him. As far as this boy knows, his presence stands in the way of his parents' happiness. Neither Mom nor Dad ever says the magic words, "I missed you."

Thoughts are never enough. How are children to know? They need to hear the words as well as see the eyes.

Ben's father goes on a date every now and then. He gets a baby sitter and steps out with Ben's mom. And they enjoy themselves.

When he comes home he makes it a point to cuddle Ben and say, "I missed you."

How long, O Lord? Will you forget me forever?
How long will you hide your face from me?...
But I trust in your unfailing love;
my heart rejoices in your salvation.
I will sing to the Lord,
for he has been good to me.

PSALM 13:1, 5-6

Watching the Clock

I can hear it ticking
On the wall.
Every second sounding off,
Every minute sliding by.

Time marching on with
Playful rhythm,
Keeping count in steady pace.
Time moving on toward
That happy moment.

My eye glances to the side.
Along the counter
I see numbers
Flashing red and green,
Each a digital reminder
That the happy moment
Is getting closer.

My wristwatch,
The car clock,
The radio
On my desk.

The bank clock.
Time and temperature
On the phone,
Dancing dots
On the VCR.

Windup, electrical
Sundial and
Battery, too.
They all
Send the same message.

The time's coming closer
When I will be
With you.

Driving the Sandhills

Like an apple tree among the trees of the forest
is my lover among the young men.
I delight to sit in his shade,
and his fruit is sweet to my taste.
He has taken me to the banquet hall,
and his banner over me is love.

SONG OF SONGS 2:3-4

This isn't for everyone, but it works for us. From time to time, early on Saturday morning we toss a few things haphazardly into the car: some fruit, a cooler with pop, a book, a newspaper, possibly a pillow.

Pat drives first. Aimlessly we drive through the quiet sandhills of Nebraska. Rolling along Highway 2 or Route 11 we amble along, driving with neither destiny nor agenda. First, Bill reads the paper. Then he falls asleep. When Bill wakes up, Pat calls his attention to the North Loup River stretching its way lazily across a hidden valley.

Occasionally we fiddle with the radio. A bit of Public Radio here, a little country music there. Later we pick out a favorite tape or two.

Two or three hours later we pull off to look at something. Or else we stop to look at nothing. We climb a rock. We ford a stream. We trek through trees. Once in a while we hold hands, but that's risky business at any age.

We might stop at an old fort or check out an abandoned chalk mine. There is only one rule. We have to be aimless. Aimlessness means we probably won't get anywhere. That's exactly the point. We don't *want* to get anywhere.

Eventually we find a small cafe. It might be in the middle of town, on the square. It might be beside a highway, so far off the beaten path that only the truly aimless would ever venture in to find a delicious home-cooked meal. The best cafes are discovered accidentally, like gold.

The only real danger in outings like this is that one person—and maybe two—might get a tad too touchy-feely. Married couples, even couples who've been married quite a while, can get a little foolish if they take long, aimless rides.

So if you follow our advice some weekend and start out early to drive in the Nebraska sandhills along Route 11, be alert. If you see a compact white car parked by a roadside picnic area late in the afternoon under the trees, do us a favor. Keep on driving.

We probably didn't park there so we could draw a crowd.

Do You Remember When?

Whoso loves
Believes the impossible.
ELIZABETH BARRETT BROWNING

We walked along the Tidal Basin when cherry trees were in bloom. That early spring we barely knew each other, but we wanted to. We stood beside Jefferson's and Lincoln's monuments and dreamed of what might become. Love was budding, and we dared to follow wherever it might lead.

A wedding was held. The minister said … something, I know not what. Then we were off to our honeymoon in the Pocono Mountains, wrapped in each other's love. I don't remember if we went hiking or sightseeing, or if we haunted flea markets. Did I mention that we were wrapped in each other's love?

The early lessons of marriage were learned in graduate school. An efficiency apartment, empty pockets, experimental meals were our teachers. Young love covered a multitude of indignities. We learned, we grew and we hung on. Hanging on was very important.

Soon came the visits to delivery rooms. The place

where real miracles come true. You were brave. You were exhausted. You were so easy to love. Never were you tougher than the time we didn't make it to the hospital and you delivered in the car.

God was good. We believed. We worked. We shared. Our dreams came true, even those once-in-a-while times when we thought it might all fall apart. We rushed children to emergency rooms and survived auto accidents. We cried for our children and we buried our parents.

Once in a great while we wanted to leave. But are we ever glad we didn't.

Do you remember all of that?

Today the love story goes on. Of course, we've aged a bit since cherry blossom time. Snow on the roof, wrinkles farther down. I take medicine I swore I'd never take, and the knees talk to me when I stand up.

Did I mention that we still get wrapped in each other's love?

Standing by the Radio

Next to the love of God, the love of country is the best preventive of crime.

GEORGE BORROW

It may not be all that cool anymore, but there was a time. There was a time when we stood erect in ballparks and sang along when the national anthem played. Men removed their hats. Hands covered hearts. Eyes sparkled with pride.

There was a time when children stood as the band struck up "The Star Spangled Banner" on the radio. Boys saluted. Girls placed their hands on hearts. No one told them to. Their respect for country came naturally and without question.

Most of those boys and girls from another era maintained that sense of identity as they grew. Their spirits still quicken at the sight of the red, white and blue flapping in the wind. They still get lumps in their throats when they hear the national anthem.

A lot has happened over the decades. Soldiers have died. Scandals have paraded across the headlines. Corruption has rusted out government pillars here and there. Our nation has taken a few hits. Some of them we deserved, many we did not.

Our nation is still growing up and maybe it always will. We are still learning about important things: how to get along with those unlike ourselves in race or religion, how to handle responsibly our cultural legacies of free speech and world power. Every once in a while we need to remind ourselves of the courage demonstrated by so many that made these lessons possible.

Some days we hang our heads and feel a little ashamed. We wonder how we could let our country do this or that. But then we forgive ourselves and we reach out again for the good. Because as a nation we have accomplished so many fine things.

We pick up our heads again, because we must. With one hand we embrace our past, and with the other we reach out for a better, stronger tomorrow. And as we do, we dream of the day when little boys and girls, and men and women from all walks of life, will salute the flag as they stand in the halls of justice and be very proud that they love their country.

He that gives should never remember,
he that receives should never forget.

TALMUD

The Gift of Laughter

Be happy, young man, while you are young, and let your heart give you joy in the days of your youth.

ECCLESIASTES 11:9a

One didn't have to eavesdrop to hear the lady. I didn't have to crane my neck or cup my ear to pick up a muffled word or two. Minding my own business I could easily enjoy her pleasant, lilting voice. "Try this one."

We were all in an upscale department store. The woman's husband, fifty-five years old or so, was trying on jackets. "The sizes in these coats must be wrong," he joked. "This one says 32, but it doesn't fit at all. Maybe I should try a 34."

He slid his right arm into another garment.

"Well," the lady chimed in good-naturedly, "maybe you should try a 36 if having it wrap all the way around you is important."

Both husband and wife grinned as they playfully bantered back and forth. This middle-aged couple sounded like teenagers kidding each other on a first date.

Many couples lose their laughter. Life becomes serious, bills become burdensome, children have needs, decisions loom large. The challenges of living together sometimes seem difficult to endure. And yet, some couples still keep a twinkle in their eyes, a sparkle in their voices and humor in their tone.

Love without humor is possible. But it's like wheels without rubber. Bumps hit harder, noises bang louder and the trip wears us out.

Laughter is good medicine. Smart couples take it twice daily, washed down with fruit juice. When humor goes, a relationship is in for forty miles of bad road.

Always laugh when you can; it is a cheap medicine. Merriment is a philosophy not well understood. It is the sunny side of existence.

LORD BYRON

If I Were Twenty-One Again

For a crowd is not company;
and faces are but a gallery of pictures;
and talk but a tinkling cymbal,
where there is no love.

FRANCIS BACON

People who have been married a long time have learned something about love. We have an idea of what it is and what it is not. So I wondered what would happen if I could go back and start all over. How would I fall in love if I were twenty-one again?

First of all I would pay attention to looks. I know that's the wrong answer, but I would. Not Hollywood looks, but looks that draw me. Looks that I could dream about. A face that haunts me. A smile that draws me like a tack to a magnet. "Love is a great beautifier," wrote Louisa May Alcott. On the other hand, if I cannot think of that person as good-looking, then the love bug cannot bite.

Second, I would look for self-respect. Not conceit or arrogance but someone who respects herself. A person who believes her feelings count. That person thinks that the feelings of others count, too.

Third, I would look for someone who is sexy. Sorry. I know that's also not very spiritual-sounding. But let's get real. If I am not interested in eventually going to bed with this person, I need to ask why. Sex is a natural process. If I think, "I love using computers with her, but I wouldn't want to actually hold her," maybe I would be happier joining a computer club.

Fourth, I'd look for a person who feels we are equal. I don't need someone who has to prove she is smarter (but I would appreciate it if she could help me spell).

Fifth, faith would be important to that person. We need to agree that God cares for us and can do something in our lives. That's basic Theology 101. Faith can make a difference on the rocky road of this life as well as the next.

What I would look for is quite simple. With these few ingredients we could bake a good cake. Most of the other things are just frosting, candles and fancy lettering.

I'll tell you one more thing. Even when we don't know what is best for us, God always gives more than we could have imagined for ourselves. I only have to look at Pat to know this. I didn't know exactly what I was looking for the first time, but I got all the basics anyway!

Part Two:

True Love Is Healing

But I tell you: Love your enemies and pray for those who persecute you, that you may be sons of your Father in heaven.

JESUS CHRIST
MATTHEW 5:44-45a

Tea for Two

We pardon to the extent that we love.

FRANÇOIS ROCHEFOUCAULD

Their favorite thing to do each Saturday evening was to spread out a tablecloth and tea set on the back porch. Mother and young daughter watched the sun sink slowly behind the trees as they ate real cookies and drank pretend tea.

Sipping slowly, pinkie fingers raised high, they talked about make-believe people. Mrs. Gigglepuff who ran a boarding school was created in their active minds. Mr. Bossman, the one-legged fisherman, had exciting adventures.

Mother never mentioned her divorced husband while they socialized in the evening. The seven-year-old girl chose not to bring up the father who never came around. They just engaged in girl talk. A visitor would never have guessed that something or some-one was missing.

Too soon the teen years came when mother and daughter no longer pretended. They never again sat on the back porch. They seldom talked. When they did, their conversations often ended in loud, harsh voices and slamming doors.

Six months before graduation, the daughter left

town with a twenty-two-year-old. Mother thinks they headed north, but she isn't sure. In the years that have followed she has received a postcard now and then. Each time the postmark bears the name of another town. Twice she has received brief phone calls.

Maybe tomorrow will be different. Her daughter might settle down. Sometimes Mother dreams her child might move back. Not to the same house but just a few blocks away.

Sitting on the back porch in the evening Mother looks at the rickety furniture and remembers: A smiling face, the tilted cup, the tall pitcher. She remembers the happy days and she is grateful. Grateful for every day they hung together and showed each other love.

It could happen again. But then again it might not. And if it doesn't, Mother will play the tape over in her mind and be thankful for the little girl she used to know.

You will call and I will answer you;
you will long for the creature your hands have
  made.
Surely then you will count my steps
but not keep track of my sin.

JOB 14:15-16

Love is the only fire

against which there is no insurance.

You Can Count on Me

You can give without loving,
but you cannot love without giving.

AMY CARMICHAEL

Darling, I want you to know,

When someone yells at you at work, when the thoughtless boss blames you, or when you finish the big report and no one thanks you,

You can count on me.

When the school principal calls to ask if you realize that our Cody is bringing worms to school, and the little genius is putting those worms in Mrs. Lungren's top desk drawer,

You can count on me.

When your brother-in-law wants to borrow a thousand dollars because he wants to hang out at Turtle Beach until he "finds himself,"

You can count on me.

When the bank calls to say we are overdrawn because you forgot to write down the last three checks,

You can count on me.

When you are tired of trying because no one in the family seems to appreciate anything you do, and when you feel like the term "thank you" has been banned from the planet,

You can count on me.

Because I have
a strong feeling,
an inner feeling,
even a firm conviction
that "you can count on me"
really means
I love you.

And now these three remain:

faith,

hope

and love.

But the greatest of these is love.

1 CORINTHIANS 13:13

Here's My Heart

Many people when they fall in love look for a little haven of refuge from the world, where they can be sure of being admired when they are not admirable, and praised when they are not praiseworthy.

BERTRAND RUSSELL

Here's my heart.
Handle it with care.
My heart bruises
Far too easily.
And when it bruises,
It takes a long, long time
To heal again.

Here's my heart.
I don't offer it lightly
Because I'd hate to see
It get hurt again.
Securely it hides
Deep inside my chest,
Deep beneath my ribs,
Leery of everyone.

Here's my heart.
I have now decided
To give it all to you
Without reservation, without regret.
The only freedom
My heart will ever know
Will be the fresh air
It can find with you.

Here's my heart.
Handle it with care.
For now I finally know
You will keep it close.
And it will be
A better heart
For every day
You hold it
Next to yours.

Love does not delight in evil but rejoices with the truth. It always protects, always trusts, always hopes, always perseveres.

1 CORINTHIANS 13:6-7

Mother Came Back

*Who can guess how much industry and providence
and affection we have caught from the pantomime
of brutes?*

RALPH WALDO EMERSON

Having dabbled with nature, I have never
become strongly attached to it. Hiking is fun,
standing by a waterfall is a kick, but I have sworn to
never sleep on the ground again the rest of my life. I
don't eat bark or look for slugs. Nature is a place I
like to visit. We respect each other.

Standing near a tree after a cookout, I noticed a
baby bird lying on the prairie grass. Normally I
would have walked away and left the fledgling to its
limited devices, but two things helped change my
mind.

First, the chick was a bit advanced and showed
promise of survival. Second, and most compelling,
several children from camp stood around, wondering
what I would do next.

"If we touch it to put it back in its nest," I announced in a semi-scientific tone, "its mother will

abandon it and the chick will starve."

That's what I had been told as a child. Unfortunately the four or five pairs of eyes staring at me didn't seem to care about the axiom. Their faces pleaded for me to do something.

"Well," I soon gave in, "let's move a bench over here and try anyway."

Quickly hands and feet clustered around a bench and dragged it beneath a shaggy-looking nest. Gently lifting the chick and carefully climbing up, I placed the infant back into its cradle.

Mission accomplished, we put the bench back and returned to playing ball.

Shortly afterward someone shouted, "Look! The bird!"

Balls and bats dropped to the ground.

"It's the mother," someone whispered.

"She came back," another child added.

The mother bird was carrying food in her mouth to her hungry fledgling.

"She did it," someone shouted. "She fed her baby!"

Maybe the ancient saying is true. Maybe mother birds aren't supposed to come back and claim a chick after a human touches it. All we know is that this mother did.

There simply may be no accounting for how a loving mother might behave.

I call on you, O God, for you will answer me;
give ear to me and hear my prayer.
Show the wonder of your great love,
you who save by your right hand
those who take refuge in you from their foes.
Keep me as the apple of your eye;
hide me in the shadow of your wings ...

PSALM 17:6-8

Many waters cannot quench love;

rivers cannot wash it away.

SONG OF SONGS 8:7a

The Broken Bones of Friendship

One of the best things about love —
the feeling of being wrapped, like a gift,
in understanding.

ANATOLE BROYARD

Gina didn't think it was fair. When they went to lunch together Marie always, but always, selected the restaurant. If Gina suggested they try a new place, Marie was quick to offer some excuse. That restaurant was too far away, too busy, too ethnic, too expensive. Always too something.

Finally Gina blew her stack. Why was it, she exclaimed to Marie, that her idea of a restaurant was never good enough? Why was it that *she* always had to have the last word?

Stunned, Marie picked up her lunch tab, huffed a couple of times and walked away. Gina sat alone at the table, trying to accept the fact that her longtime friend had walked out.

So much for love between two friends, she thought.

Six days later Gina was still wiggling like a bewildered worm through ashes of self-pity. Finally she decided it was time to set aside her hurt.

"Why not call?" she thought. The first two or three sentences might be awkward. But maybe those stumbling steps could lead them to a bridge. And maybe that bridge might soon bring them back into a loving relationship.

Nervously, she picked up the phone.

It's the broken bone theory. Some people believe that after a bone has been broken, when it heals it is stronger than it was originally.

Sometimes love is like that. Relationships have a way of getting into trouble. People who are close often stumble, clash or trip. Too frequently, loving friends separate forever.

But every once in a while friends will bump heads hard and then bounce back. The ones who bounce back seem stronger after the break. They hang in there and heal.

Open rebuke is better
Than love carefully concealed.
Faithful are the wounds of a friend,
But the kisses of an enemy are deceitful.

PROVERBS 27:5-6 NKJV

Words That Heal

The wise in heart will be called prudent,
and sweetness of the lips increases learning....
Pleasant words are like a honeycomb,
sweetness to the soul and health to the bones.

PROVERBS 16:21, 24

Leslie had never thought about the words she used when she talked to her children and her husband. Never considered how those words sounded, or the emotional weight behind them.

It never occurred to her, that is, until one evening in January at a local discount store. There Leslie saw a woman who appeared to be slightly older than herself roughly grab a small girl by the arm. "Stay here! You're acting like a little ..."

Stunned, Leslie could hardly believe her ears. How could a mother say that to such a beautiful young child? As quickly as she thought it, she recoiled with a shameful memory. Not so long ago, she had said the same thing to her own child.

Driving home, Leslie wondered what else she had said to her family. Ugly words. Mean words. Thoughtless words. Cruel words. She felt her face grow warm with embarrassment as she heard her own voice on the tape player in her mind.

Words create atmosphere. Kind and caring words bring love and healing. Mean and ugly words wound and injure. Some words raise tempers and keep people on edge. Other words calm and allow peace to prevail.

We deceive ourselves by saying, "Oh, she knows I'm just kidding." In fact she might know nothing of the kind. Some of us have been slain by a nasty remark from a father, an aunt or a grandmother. Words have power to affect and shape us.

If we are to build a loving atmosphere, we must begin by selecting healthy words. Words that build up. Words that offer reassurance. Words that acknowledge good traits. Words that show appreciation. Words that speak of love and acceptance.

Going places together, spending time together, playing together all have value if they are accompanied by words of hope. Words of encouragement. Words of faith. Words of love.

Hatred stirs up dissension,
but love covers over all wrongs.

PROVERBS 10:12

If angry, count to ten before you speak.

If very angry, to one hundred.

THOMAS JEFFERSON

Part Three:

True Love Knows No Limits

There is no fear in love.

But perfect love drives out fear,

because fear has to do with punishment.

The one who fears is not made perfect in love.

1 JOHN 4:18

Love in a Concentration Camp

Those who sow in tears
will reap with songs of joy.
He who goes out weeping,
carrying seed to sow,
will return with songs of joy,
carrying sheaves with him.

PSALM 126:5-6

Dr. Viktor Frankl spent years in a concentration camp. His life continuously hung in the balance. At any moment he could have been shot and his body burned to ashes. And yet, somehow he found the inner strength to go on. Where did it come from? How did he survive under such treatment?

One of Dr. Frankl's keys to hope was thinking of his beloved wife. In his mind's eye he could see her warm, smiling face. Other prisoners expressed similar visions about their wives and other loved ones. Working under harsh conditions, dragging themselves through mud and ice, each prisoner was in a real sense kept alive by the person who lived in his heart and mind.

Later Frankl wrote in *Man's Search for Meaning:*

"I understood how a man who has nothing left in this world may still know bliss, be it only for a brief moment, in the contemplation of his beloved."

Love for someone can become a well from which we draw comfort and strength. In illness we seek out the face of the one we love. Under pressure we imagine the moment when we will hold each other again. We take the high road in moral choices because we care more for that other person than we care about any selfish gain.

Fortunate is the person who can draw on this inner strength. Courage can give us determination. Faith may shield us from foolish decisions made in haste. But it is love that gives us hope. The desire to speak to, touch, comfort and show love to another person gives us purpose and focus.

Blessed is the person who reaches out and loves someone.

*With love one can live
even without happiness.*
FYODOR DOSTOYEVSKY

To you, O Lord, I lift up my soul;

in you I trust, O my God....

No one whose hope is in you

will ever be put to shame....

Show me your ways, O Lord,

teach me your paths;

guide me in your truth and teach me,

for you are my God and my Savior,

and my hope is in you all day long.

PSALM 25:1-5

When two people achieve lasting happiness, this is not solely because they are great lovers but because they are also—I must put it crudely—good people; controlled, loyal, fair-minded, mutually adaptable people.

C.S. LEWIS

What Is Love?

Dear friends, since God so loved us, we also ought to love one another.

1 JOHN 4:11

Love is listening to Uncle Sam's story that you have heard a dozen times. You listen anyway, one more time, just to see the gleam in his eyes. You give him the joy of spinning that tale again.

Love is calling your mother even if you are not feeling well. You draw cheerfulness to you and dial the number because she will be expecting a call.

Love sits through a slow movie because your friend wants to see this one. Love quietly eats popcorn. Love sits still while the music drones on and dialogues crawl across endless lawns, through gardens, past hedges, along the lines of weeping willows and cottonless cottonwoods. Because she wants to be there.

Love watches while Butler tackles Griffith, and Brett passes the ball to Deion, and Reggie smashes the quarterback flat. Love buys extra chips and dip, and never mentions your stressed-out waistline or bulging jeans. And when the running back gets a concussion, love acts like this must be something good.

Love goes to the park, crosses bridges and walks nature trails because your nephew loves it. Love flies kites, eats watermelon and has seed-spitting contests.

Love lets her pick out the wallpaper.

Love leaves him undisturbed for an entire evening at the computer.

Love lets her cry when he can't figure out why.

Love lets him get uptight and gives him space.

Love doesn't always defend its rights. Because love is more than something we get. First and foremost love is something we give.

I try to give to the poor for love what the rich could get for money.
No, I wouldn't touch a leper for a thousand pounds; yet I willingly cure him for the love of God.

MOTHER TERESA

No One Might Know

The growing good of the world is partly dependent on unhistoric acts; and that things are not so ill with you and me as they might have been, is half owing to the number who lived faithfully a hidden life, and rest in unvisited tombs.

GEORGE ELIOT

Whenever I go to visit my nephew, I know it's only a matter of time before I hear, "Let's go to the park!" Less than a mile away is the center of his four-year-old universe: Wooden City, the mother of all jungle gyms. Swings and slides, dangle bars and cubbyholes galore … built for the children of the community by civic-minded folks.

Hand in hand, we skip up to the gate and lose ourselves in the swarm of crawling and climbing hands and feet. On benches nearby, parents chat quietly as animated chaos ensues. A pleasant-looking gentleman in overalls strolls by the fence and smiles at us. I wonder how many of these post holes he dug himself, and smile back.

Every town has these nameless do-gooders who make the world a better place for us. Let's send up a quiet prayer of thanksgiving for those who, having never met us, are leaving behind a loving legacy for us to enjoy.

First, a word of thanks to people who worked hard to help those less fortunate than themselves. Some built parks in hot, crowded cities so we could play instead of getting into trouble. Others gave us free trips to camp each summer so we could swim in the bay, catch sea nettles and tell stories by a fire. And thank God for the forgotten heroes who opened doors so the poor, minorities and women could get educations. They endured great resistance to help people they would never meet.

Let's remember the ones who fought spiritual poverty as well. We should especially remember those who decided to build a church just down the street from where we would one day live. They planned and prayed and sacrificed so the generations that followed could hear about the grace of Jesus Christ. And let's not forget those who worked hard to serve the church *after* it was built: Sunday school teachers, janitors and the ladies who baked cookies for snack time at vacation Bible school every summer.

Thanks to those in the medical profession, who labored diligently to develop medicines so that seriously ill babies and children might live. A special word of thanks to those who agreed to be "guinea pigs" at the testing stages, knowing full well that they themselves might not be cured.

Many of these unsung heroes gave up wealth and prestige, and endured unspeakable hardships. They lost homes, lands and jobs; they endured loneliness, suffering and deprivation. They left their countries and died in wars to provide for people they loved—and yet would never see. As we remember them, their acts of kindness continue to live on for—and in—us.

Greater love has no one than this,
that he lay down his life for his friends.

JOHN 15:13

Drink water from your own cistern,

running water from your own well.

Should your springs overflow in the streets,

your streams of water in the public squares?

Let them be yours alone,

never to be shared with strangers.

May your fountain be blessed,

and may you rejoice in the wife of your

youth.

A loving doe, a graceful deer—

may her breasts satisfy you always,

may you ever be captivated by her love.

PROVERBS 5:15-19

He Chose NOT to Love

Those who belong to Christ Jesus have crucified the sinful nature with its passions and desires. Since we live by the Spirit, let us keep in step with the Spirit.

GALATIANS 5:24-25

Five days a week Curt ate lunch at 12:30 in a small back room at the factory. He ate alone. Except for one other person, that is. Her name was Angie.

Angie was a little younger than Curt. She was bright and energetic. She was also single. Curt, on the other hand, was married and had a two-year-old girl. And yet, Curt seldom mentioned his wife as he rummaged through a lunch pail and she ate a sandwich.

Angie laughed at Curt's jokes. That made him feel good. She also asked him for advice. She thought he was wise. Their conversations were always innocent. Basically they talked about things she could share with no one else, and about subjects his wife never had time to hear.

They talked. They kidded. They smiled. And every so often their eyes met. At first their eyes met and turned away. Then their eyes began to meet and linger just a bit.

One cold Tuesday in the middle of March Curt did not show up at lunch time. He didn't show up on Wednesday. He didn't show up on Thursday, or Friday either.

The following Monday Angie saw Curt eating lunch high up on a ledge overlooking the plant. She waved but he made no effort to come down.

The week before Curt had had a heart-to-heart talk with himself. It was time to grow up. Time to take charge of his own feelings. It was time to fall back in love with his wife. Never again did Curt's eyes look into Angie's. Curt made a choice. He decided to go back and love the woman who owned his heart.

Has not the Lord made them one? In flesh and spirit they are his. And why one? Because he was seeking godly offspring. So guard yourself in your spirit, and do not break faith with the wife of your youth.

MALACHI 2:15

A successful marriage
is one in which you fall in love many times,
always with the same person.

MIGNON MCLAUGHLIN

Love Says No

When someone asks us
To go somewhere
And we don't feel good
About going,
Love says No.

When someone close
Wants us to prove
How much we love
By giving in,
Love says No.

Love knows how
To draw lines,
Set limits,
And keep its own standards.

Love is careful
To give
What's worth giving
And keep
What's worth keeping.
And love
Knows the difference.

When someone dares us
To prove our love
By doing something dumb
Or by compromising,
Love says No.

Love is saying Yes.
Love is saying Maybe.
Love is saying Wait.
And Love is saying
No way.

Because of Love ...

Then the righteous will answer him, "Lord, when did we see you hungry and feed you, or thirsty and give you something to drink? When did we see you a stranger and invite you in, or needing clothes and clothe you? When did we see you sick or in prison and go to visit you?"

The King will reply, "I tell you the truth, whatever you did for one of the least of these brothers of mine, you did for me."

MATTHEW 25:37-40

The flickering image on the television captured my undivided attention. There was Lillian Carter holding a little girl with leprosy in her arms. After saying a few words, she kissed the girl—on the lips—before gently setting her on the ground.

I don't recall what she said next. But I'll never forget that kiss. I doubt the little girl will, either. And yet, that kiss also reminded me that there are all kinds of people, all over the world, who are doing amazing things just because of love.

Because of love a minister in Indianapolis hugged a gay man after his best friend's funeral service.

Because of love an Asian lady at a shelter sang a lullaby to a scared little Mexican girl.

Because of love a pregnant woman decided to keep her child, no matter what. And the next day, because of love her father in Seattle welcomed her home.

Because of love your mother sat in a chair and rocked you through the night. Years later, because of love someone left cash in the mailbox at your college dorm.

Because of love your spouse forgave you for giving away his favorite shirt. And because of love you'll forgive him for leaving up the toilet seat ... again.

Because of love a baby was born two thousand years ago, and was placed in a manger to sleep. In time, that baby grew up to be a man. Because of love Jesus died and rose again ... and is coming back to take us to be with him forever.

What would *you* do ... just because of love?

Part Four:

True Love in the Making

There is nothing more contrary to our wicked nature than this loving our neighbor as ourselves. Wee can with ease envie him if he be rich, or scorne him if he be poore; but love him?

ELIZABETH JACOLINE

The Three Big R's of Love

Home is the place where, when you go there,
they have to take you in.

ROBERT FROST

Love is best if you grow up with it. You become used to seeing love at the breakfast table or watching it up close working in the yard together. Happy is the person whose parents had kindness in their eyes and laughter in their voices.

Brad hadn't had that privilege. His parents never cared for each other and didn't hide their disdain. When he married the youthful Marianne, his love was awkward, uneasy and often impolite.

Quickly Marianne understood the considerable task before her. She would have to open a school and teach a grown man what love is and how it operates. No simple task to be sure, but Marianne preferred it over any of the alternatives.

Looking for a place to start, she chose the three R's. The lesson plan went: Respect, Romance and Repetition. If her approach wasn't perfect, it was her best try.

Respect. Her opinion was as good as his, and his was as good as hers. One would not put the other down, and anything that sounded demeaning had to be corrected immediately. Her Bible often spoke of respect, and Marianne knew there would be only friction without it.

Romance. Brad would have to learn more about how to say loving things, how to make love and how to plan a good date. No more gorilla mentality at bedtime. It's a lot more fun, she told him, if both partners are ready and willing.

Repetition. Marianne didn't expect Brad to graduate from college in one weekend. He was going to miss some points. He was bound to forget. That's where her steady teaching skills would come in handy. "Good try, Brad," she would say, "but let's try it again."

Marianne wanted a better love, not a new one. That's why she took Brad to school.

The fruit of the Spirit is love …

GALATIANS 5:22

The greatest pleasure I know is to do a good action by stealth, and to have it found out by accident.

CHARLES LAMB

Words of Love

Thank you.

Please.

I'm glad you're here.

Would you like some?

Let me get it for you.

I like your jacket.

I'm sorry.

How can I help?

Tell me about it.

How does that make you feel?

Thought for the Day:

"You have the most beautiful eyes in the world," she sighs.

She knows she is lying. You know she's lying. And you both eat it up.

I Never Loved

Love comes hard
to some of us
who treat it
as a foe.

We fear
that love will
someday
run away.

But it is better
to have loved
and tried,
to have loved
and cried,
than never to
have loved at all.

So never again
can I say
I never loved.
For I love you
From this day on.

A Dozen Loving Things
Every Child Needs to Hear

1. I love you exactly the way you are.
2. You are a wonderful gift from God.
3. I love doing things with you.
4. When you do something wrong, I still love you.
5. Because I love you I will sometimes take away privileges.
6. Love means I will not call you ugly names.
7. Love means I will not lie to you.
8. Because I love you, you can count on me to take care of you.
9. I promise to listen to what you have to say (but sometimes not at that moment).
10. I love you, but I will make mistakes.
11. I do not love your brother or sister more than you.
12. Because I love you, I promise to forgive you.

I believe that love is stronger than death.

ROBERT FULGHUM

When you get into a tight place and everything goes against you, till it seems as though
you could not hold on a minute longer, never
give up then, for that is just the place and time
that the tide will turn.

HARRIET BEECHER STOWE

Some Mothers Fake It

*Can a mother forget the baby at her breast and have
no compassion on the child she has borne? Though she
may forget, I will not forget you! See, I have en-
graved you on the palms of my hands....*

ISAIAH 49:15-16

There are some women for whom motherhood
does not come naturally. In a way, they deserve
a special tribute. Perhaps they never experienced an
outpouring of affection from their own mothers. Or
maybe it just never occurred to them how good it
might feel to scoop little Sally and Joey Junior to
their bosom and love the dickens out of them.

Mothers for whom the act of nurturing is labor,
pure and simple, are not evil or distorted in char-
acter. Unfortunately, they just have the mothering
instincts of an asparagus stalk.

If you know a mother like that—if *your* mother
was like that—you may want to stand up for one
moment and salute her anyway. For she did what
did not come naturally. She held her child, bathed
the tiny dear and rocked her baby late into the
night merely because it had to be done. Her sense

of dedication and duty pulled the maternal wagon where instincts failed to kick in. The joy of parenting never seemed to bubble over, but her loyalty and protective spirit filled in the gaps.

Those mothers had to do it the hard way. And a fine job they have done. They never felt ecstasy in building Tinkertoys or pushing swings. They did what had to be done, and no child of theirs was ever neglected.

Lined up along the altar on Dedication Sunday, six parents in a row, who can tell the difference? Each mom cradles a baby in her arms with a warm look on her face. Who can say which ones naturally love being a mother, and which find it an endless chore? Their secret is safe with us.

Let this be a tribute to that mother here or there who doesn't come by it naturally. But she does it anyway.

> *We can do no great things—*
> *only small things with great love.*
>
> MOTHER TERESA

More Words of Love

Show me what you made.

You did a good job.

You mean a lot to me.

I'll pray for you.

Excuse me.

I love doing things with you.

I'm in no hurry.

I missed you.

Where would you like to eat?

I'll drive.

Let me pay.

Part Five:

Love Busters and Menders

Love is life. All, everything I understand, I understand only because I love. Everything is, everything that exists, only because I love. Everything is united by it alone.

LEO TOLSTOY

Let no debt remain outstanding, except the continuing debt to love one another, for he who loves his fellowman has fulfilled the law. The commandments, "Do not commit adultery," "Do not murder," "Do not steal," "Do not covet," and whatever other commandment there may be, are summed up in this one rule: "Love your neighbor as yourself." Love does no harm to its neighbor. Therefore love is the fulfillment of the law.

ROMANS 13:8-10

Love Maintenance

The wise woman builds her house, but with her own hands the foolish one tears hers down.

PROVERBS 14:1

Cars are hard to love if you grew up in a city, without a vehicle, as I did. Transportation meant buses and streetcars. There was no car to park or license. No hood to lift. No tires to kick. No oil to check.

With that kind of background, a car was a genuine mystery to me. What an engine was supposed to do or exactly how brakes worked were too much to figure out. Initially my approach was simply to drive. If a noise was loud or the engine stopped running, I begrudgingly found a mechanic.

Eventually I purchased a brand-new car. Fresh from the factory, this vehicle had no flaws. No clanging, no jumps and starts, no squeaks. And as if by magic, this owner gained a new attitude. I began to give the car proper maintenance. Changed the oil, checked the fluids, even periodically measured the antifreeze. Thirteen years later, it still runs great; there are 260,000 miles on the odometer.

That car taught me a valuable lesson: When we

care about something, we try to meet its needs. When we meet something's needs, we are much more likely to love it.

When I got married, I discovered that the same rules that apply to cars apply to love. The truth is, I didn't understand love at first. I thought you could ignore love and it would take care of itself. As long as there wasn't excessive racket or too many complaints, what else did love need?

After a few misfires, a shouting match or two, and too many nights sleeping on the couch, it dawned on me. Love, like every important thing, requires maintenance. A little listening here, a bit of understanding there, a compliment each day. Love, to remain love, needs to be cared for. To keep love vital each person has to "tune up the engine" on a regular basis.

He who is in love is wise and is becoming wiser, sees newly every time he looks at the object beloved, drawing from it with his eyes and his mind those virtues which it possesses.

RALPH WALDO EMERSON

If I gave everything I have to poor people, and if I were burned alive for preaching the Gospel But didn't love others, it would be of no value whatever.

1 CORINTHIANS 13:3 TLB

This is the message we have heard from him and declare to you: God is light; in him there is no darkness at all. If we claim to have fellowship with him yet walk in darkness, we lie and do not live by the truth. But if we walk in the light, as he is in the light, we have fellowship with one another, and the blood of Jesus, his Son, purifies us from all sin.

1 JOHN 1:5-7

Don't Blow Out the Candles

There is no more lovely, friendly, or charming relationship, communion or company, than a good marriage.
MARTIN LUTHER

At a recent wedding I wanted to stand up in the middle of the ceremony and shout, "Stop! Stop!" Fortunately, I restrained the impulse—even with my primitive social skills I knew better than to do that. But I wanted to.

The service had reached the point where the bride and groom lighted a tall, white "unity" candle to demonstrate that they are now one. So far so good. Being one is an excellent idea. But then they blew out their individual candles, as though they were puffing themselves out. It gave me the jitters.

Can't the bride and groom become one person without extinguishing themselves? Can't there really be three people in a marriage? You, Me and Us?

Love at its best should allow Me to become a better Me. That same benefit should be afforded to my spouse. Love does not squelch, shrink or diminish either of us. And the better the You and Me are, the better the Us will be.

True love demands sacrifice on the part of each. However, love also stimulates and invigorates. Love promotes dreams. Love sets us free. Love dares us to stretch our wings and fly. Love was never designed to snuff anyone out.

Love frees us up to give, to help, to provide, to care, to share who we really are. Love will expand our possibilities and allow our personalities to ride new waves.

Who wants to snuff out the candle? No loving husband wants his wife to become less. No loving wife wants her husband to stop being him. Love gives life. In marriage two people do become one flesh, but they remain two people. When they get up in the morning, one can still choose pineapple juice while the other pours grapefruit.

At the next wedding the bride and groom should be a bit nervous. I might be sitting in the congregation. And when they light the unity candle and bring their own candles up to their lips, I just might forget my inadequate manners.

Love creates an
"us" without
destroying a "me."

LEO BUSCAGLIA

Hawaii on a Budget

Better a little with the fear of the Lord
than great wealth with turmoil.
Better a meal of vegetables where there is love
than a fattened calf with hatred.

PROVERBS 15:16-17

Rick's business had great potential. It had potential sales, potential profits, potential growth and potential long-term security. The problem was that his computer store was in its third year of potential. So far revenues had only trickled in. There was enough to pay the bills, but nothing for extras.

During their eight years of marriage, Judy had often wished for a trip to Hawaii, a second honeymoon. She dreamed of ocean breezes, soft music and sand between her toes. She envisioned walking with Rick on the beach, arm in arm, under the moonlight.

But what hope was there? Credit was strained to the max. A pricey trip across the Pacific was unthinkable. But love began to look for a way. Rick sat down and had a frank talk with his heart and his imagination.

Almost magically a plan began to take shape.

Two weeks later, he invited his loving wife on a secret date. No questions, he told her. No answers.

No discussion. Just be in the car and bring a change of clothes.

Suspicious and giddy, Judy did as she was told.

Parking at a comfortable motel in a nearby city, Rick led his apprehensive wife to Room 219. He covered Judy's eyes, and they stepped cautiously into the room. Judy heard Pacific Island music and the sound of breaking waves in the background.

Opening her eyes, Judy saw large Hawaii travel posters along the walls, leis draping the furniture, and a beautiful buffet with fresh pineapples on the table.

"I hope this will do until I can afford the big trip," Rick told his speechless wife. "I love you."

O lyric Love, half angel and half bird
And all a wonder and a wild desire.

ROBERT BROWNING

Emotional Pack Rats

There seems to be a kind of order in the universe, in the movement of the stars and the turning of the earth and the changing of the seasons, and even in the cycle of human life. But human life itself is almost pure chaos. Everyone takes his stance, asserts his own rights and feelings, mistaking the motives of others and his own.

KATHERINE ANNE PORTER

Clutter creep was claiming the bedroom. Emily had set up the ironing board there because it saved her a few steps during the holidays. The sewing machine was in a nearby corner. She was sure her husband would appreciate buttons on his shirts.

Two boxes of educational materials on the floor had their purpose. While she was waiting for Randy to get ready for bed, Emily could get some of her church work done. The exercise bike, the television and the stereo contributed to a harried, driven atmosphere.

Emotional pack rats probably begin the same way. A few thoughtless words are said. Someone gets hurt over a "teasing" remark. Couples create considerable pain for each other. And too often they store bruised emotions in their hearts the same way Emily collected clutter.

Wise couples deal quickly with each emotional hit. They talk it out. They forgive. They forget. Otherwise hearts become packed with injured feelings. If we don't clean hurts out, we start to stumble. We then build up resentment. We turn to pouting, and before long find ourselves boiling over.

Smart lovers don't let their emotions pile up. They express their happiness. They voice their disappointments. They laugh at foolishness. They explain how they hurt.

The closets of our hearts are best uncluttered by airing them out.

The tongue of the righteous is choice silver,
but the heart of the wicked is of little value.
The lips of the righteous nourish many,
but fools die for lack of judgment.

PROVERBS 10:20-21

Kindness in women,

not their beauteous looks,

shall win my love.

WILLIAM SHAKESPEARE

Love, Sex and Oranges

Let him kiss me with the kisses of his mouth—
for your love is more delightful than wine.

SONG OF SONGS 1:2

In a makeshift studio just off the book convention floor, a television interviewer asked an author an important question. Barely in her twenties, she wanted to know, "What's the difference between love and sex?" Lisa deserved a good answer.

Picture orange slices side by side inside a protective blanket of peeling. Inside the cover each slice remains fresh and juicy. Tear the peeling away and immediately each part is in danger. Within hours the slices dry up and lose their appeal.

Wrapped in love, sex has the security of trust. It has the prospect of a loving future. In the relaxing world of commitment two people are free to give of themselves for more than just the moment.

"Why didn't you tell us?" a couple in their thirties wanted to know. "Why didn't you tell us how wonderful married sex is? We would have gotten married a lot sooner."

Many couples don't want to listen. They choose to believe whatever suits them for the occasion.

Often teenagers can't tell the difference between their sex drives and a heart filled with love. They imagine that if they want to sleep with a person it must be love. Many older people are just as befuddled.

Thank God for making sex so pleasurable. Frankly, it is one of his better presents to humans. At its best sex is wrapped in a broad, wide blanket of love.

Sex is too intimate to be merely left on its own. Sex is too close, too satisfying, too volatile, too threatening, too revealing, too dynamic, too encompassing to hang by itself. Even people in love have difficulties with sex. Fortunately their love for each other gives them a vital ingredient to help them work out the glitches.

Sex needs to be warmly, safely wrapped inside a blanket of love.

In this same way, husbands ought to love their wives as their own bodies. He who loves his wife loves himself.

EPHESIANS 5:28

The Pain of Parenting

Nothing is too much trouble for love.

DESMOND TUTU

Why do parents get hurt? Every mother and father go through agony with children. There is no way to love someone and not experience pain.

At first an infant gets shots from the doctor, and Mother sheds a cupful of tears. Later, the toddler falls down, bruises a knee, scratches a forehead. Mother again hurts in her heart.

That's the price of love. Love means we will care. Caring makes us sensitive. Love means we are open and vulnerable. Vulnerability means our shields are down and arrows are free to pierce our hearts.

Love wrestles over the important questions and milestones in a child's life. "Is it too soon…? Too much…? Too late…?" But love is willing to wrestle. It takes the bumps, the falls and the mat burns.

When our children become teenagers, our love becomes more complicated. Maybe their date didn't go well. Even worse, perhaps they didn't get a date at all.

Love stays awake late at night and waits. It waits for a late-night call saying they've been in an accident at Third and Bladensburg. Love waits for the door to open, even if it is three hours late. Late is better than not at all. Confrontation is preferable to wondering where they might be.

The pain of parenting should end when a child moves out or begins his own home. But we all know it doesn't. Because love is still alive. The pain never ends. A child's marriage shows some strain. A grandchild becomes sick. Jobs fold up, and the career search lasts interminably. Parents continue to feel the strain because love never stops caring.

Some people choose not to parent because they don't want to feel pain. They are free to make their own decisions, but they will be the poorer for it.

Love and pain are hand in glove. They may not be equal, but they certainly go together.

I Know What Will Help

Nothing you do for children is ever wasted. They seem not to notice us, hovering, averting our eyes, and they seldom offer thanks, but what we do for them is never wasted.

GARRISON KEILLOR

With three preschool children, Annie tried hard to be a perky, spirited mother. But on the days that came especially close on the heels of short nights, her frayed body and lack of energy were difficult to hide.

Annie worked diligently at trying to communicate with her young children. She looked at them as full people who had feelings, expectations and worthwhile needs. Her straightforward, caring approach came back to bless her one particularly stressful day.

The living room floor was a clutter, as it seemed to be most days. Her youngest child was crying and her oldest daughter was tracking mud across the kitchen floor.

Too frustrated to go on, Annie yelled at three-year-old Michael, then flopped into an overstuffed chair. Bewildered, the lad, hurt and confused, looked at his mother with compassionate brown eyes.

"I'm sorry, Michael. I guess I'm a little bit tired and sad today."

Her tone of voice begged for understanding.

Michael moved toward his frazzled mother.

"That's OK," he reassured her. "I know what will make you feel better."

Looking directly into her face, with a sparkle in his eyes, Michael announced proudly, "Mom, I love you."

Part Six:

The Many Colors of Love

Do not store up for yourselves treasures on earth, where moth and rust destroy, and where thieves break in and steal. But store up for yourselves treasures in heaven, where moth and rust do not destroy, and where thieves do not break in and steal. For where your treasure is, there your heart will be also.

MATTHEW 6:19-21

Ten Things I Love
Sharing With You

chocolate

old movies

freshly baked bread

naps

hot tub soaks

gentle music

good conversation

old poetry

sandy beaches

Chinese food

What the vast majority of American children needs is to stop being pampered, stop being indulged, stop being chauffeured, stop being catered to. In the final analysis it is not what you do for your children but what you have taught them to do for themselves that will make them successful human beings.

ANN LANDERS

Teddy Bear Love

People were bringing little children to Jesus to have him touch them, but the disciples rebuked them. When Jesus saw this, he was indignant. He said to them, "Let the little children come to me, and do not hinder them, for the kingdom of God belongs to such as these."

MARK 10:13-14

When our daughter was scheduled to go to the hospital for the birth of twins, Pat and I packed our bags to spend the night with our three-year-old grandson, Nolan. Our job this night was clearly defined. We would take care of Nolan while his parents took care of the birthing duties.

The prospect of twins had us all excited. And yet, I wondered, what does a toddler think about when two babies are about to come crying into his life? He knows things will be different, but can he even begin to imagine how? He has a lot to worry about. New people. New schedules. New tensions. New mysteries. His life will never be the same.

We took plenty of time getting Nolan ready for bed on this auspicious occasion. We played, had snacks, read books and tucked him in.

So far so good. Pat and I moved into the master

bedroom and began to settle in. Within minutes a three-year-old stood inside the doorway, clad in pajamas, holding a brown furry bear.

This wasn't *a* bear. This was *the* bear, Ted (formerly known as Teddy).

"Here. You sleep with Ted." Little outstretched arms held the present high. His generous smile was as big as his generous heart. Clearly he was concerned that Grandma and Grandpa might feel a little lonely, so far away from home.

We solemnly accepted his most valuable possession, and the four of us snuggled beneath the covers. At that moment we knew there was no need to worry. Not about Nolan, who was clearly more concerned about his grandparents feeling welcome than how his own life was about to change. And not about Nolan's parents, whose parenting skills were already reflected in their son's tender heart.

Love, in the Christian sense, does not mean an emotion. It is a state not of the feeling but of the will, that state of the will which we have naturally about ourselves, and must learn to have about other people.

C.S. LEWIS

A Love of the Game

A letter to my wife:

You may never understand my love for the game of baseball, but I'm going to try to explain. This won't be easy, but please read it through.

Why would anyone love the smell of an old baseball glove? No flower ever carried a fragrance so sweet. No symphony ever produced the tones of a ball smashing into a mitt.

No food ever tasted as delicious as a ballpark hot dog, covered with mustard and cradled inside a steaming, soft bun. All winter long your tongue longs for the taste, your nose calls out for that rich aroma.

It's even more fun when you actually get to *play*. What does it matter if you never played the game well? The dream is what counts. Every time you step up to the plate you imagine that on a good day, under the right conditions, if you lean into the ball just right, you could get lucky and smack one out of the park. In your head you hear the crack of a bat. You can almost imagine the long hit into center field and the frantic race toward first base.

It's always the dream. Someday at a picnic, at a

family choose-up game or on a back lot with grand-children, you want to steal home one more time. Imagine the fun. Tearing your trousers and scraping one knee as you slide home, hearing a volunteer umpire shout a crisp, *"Safe!"* Only missionaries and surgeons share that kind of thrill.

One fall evening as you watch the World Series on TV, the shortstop suddenly shoots deep into the hole, backhands a grounder, leaps into the air and narrowly throws out the man running to first. And you hear yourself saying to no one in particular, "I made a very similar play in the old Inner-City Church League. It was a lot like that."

No, you never quite let go of the dream.

Maybe you still don't understand it, though. Maybe you'll *never* understand it. That's OK. If you can't understand my passion for baseball, don't forget that I'll always love you at least as much as I love the game.

Your lips are like a scarlet ribbon;

your mouth is lovely.

Your temples behind your veil

are like the halves of a pomegranate.

SONG OF SONGS 4:3

Color My Love

Colors, like features,
follow the changes of the emotions.

PABLO PICASSO

Recently I was working with children who had been touched by a divorce. Realizing how limiting words can be, I asked each child to draw a circle, then color inside the circle to show me what divorce looks like.

One child filled the entire page completely in black. Another used a mixture of colors to convey both the good and bad that came with his parents' divorce. A third child used only light colors, depicting cheerful, hopeful aspects that divorce brought to her life.

As adults we try—sometimes we try too hard—to verbalize each feeling, to articulate each emotion. And yet, sometimes colors express feelings more clearly than words can. So next time you find yourself using the same old words and meaningless clichés, why not try something a little different?

What is the color of your love? Draw a circle, and pick up those crayons.

How does it feel when the phone rings and you hope it's that special person on the other end of the line?

Take a risk. Fill in the circle.

What color is your circle at the end of a long day, when you know that the person you love most in the world is home, waiting to see you again?

Go ahead. Color it in.

What about when your schedules are so loaded that you don't see each other until long after the kids are in bed? What color is your circle then?

Be brave. Fill in the circle with whichever colors you feel express your love most clearly. Vibrant reds. Rich greens. Moody purples. Gloomy blacks.

But don't just fill in a solid color--think of textures and shading as well. How much should be dark, and how much light? How often do the colors follow a pattern? Do they swirl to demonstrate energy, even vitality? The colors in the circle are limited only by your imagination. Don't draw pictures. The point is color and only color.

When you are done, sit beside your partner and take turns discussing your drawings. The other person might see messages in the colors which you, the artist, did not see.

See your love in a new way. Grow from the experience.

Love the Lord your God

with all your heart

and with all your soul

and with all your mind

and with all your strength.

JESUS CHRIST
MARK 12:30

Ten More Things I Love
Sharing With You

a well-worn chair

my favorite shirt

apple butter

soft rain

summer breezes

shady trees

slow walks

hooting owls

being snowed in

a crackling fireplace

a positive dental checkup

He who does not mind his belly, will hardly mind anything else.

SAMUEL JOHNSON

Do not worry, saying, "What shall we eat?" or "What shall we drink?" or "What shall we wear?" For the pagans run after all these things, and your heavenly Father knows that you need them. But seek first his kingdom and his righteousness, and all these things will be given to you as well.

MATTHEW 6:31-33

I Love Donuts

There is no love sincerer than the love of food.

GEORGE BERNARD SHAW

This may not sound intellectual. In the context of nutrition it may not sound wise. It certainly isn't the kind of thing you would want to stand up and say in church: "Thank God for donuts."

But the fact remains, my body craves those round, soft pieces of dough with sprinkles on top. I love donuts.

Don't tell me how harmful they are. I don't want to know their calorie count or sugar content. Not a word about how they will pick up your energy for about an hour and then drop you like a rock. The only fact I really accept is that I love donuts.

What do they go best with? How about hot coffee in the morning on the way to work? You arrive with burnt lips, sugar droppings on your clothes and icing on your cheek.

What could taste better than cake donuts dunked in milk at bedtime? I love donuts.

Not to worry about the health risks. Merely turn that donut over so the chocolate-maple topping does not show. If we don't see the calories, they surely cannot register in our bodies, right? If bakers could design donuts to look like broccoli or carrots, we might actually receive nutritional benefits.

I love donuts. I love them without prejudice. Jelly-filled, powdered-sugared and glazed. Long johns, bear claws and apple fritters. Twists, holes and crullers. Even plain. Each and every one is accepted without reservation.

Long and thin ones.

Short and chubby ones.

Medium, large or small. (Did I mention cherry fritters?)

One at a time, or a dozen to go.

I love donuts.

Don't tell me I don't know how to love. Don't tell me I'm cold and insensitive. And when I stand at the altar, tell the minister to simply say, "And do you take this person to have and to hold? You know, like a donut?"

I love donuts.

I love mankind —

it's people I can't stand!

LINUS

Never Fall in Love With ...

Love covers over a multitude of sins.

1 PETER 4:8

love	gambling
sleep	other people's spouses
movie stars	spiders
pecan pie	smooth talkers
your own voice	sashaying women
fast cars	2:00 A.M.
alcohol	adrenaline
depression	your own mirror
medicine	tight jeans
your own rights	tighter jeans
loud music	flattery
spending	German chocolate cake
deception	television
tobacco	psychics

The Man Who Loved Poetry

All good poetry is the spontaneous overflow of power-ful feelings: it takes its origin from emotion recollect-ed in tranquillity.

WILLIAM WORDSWORTH

Bright-eyed and disheveled, a thirty-five-year-old man stood conspicuously in Central Park. With papers bundled under one arm, he read loudly from a single sheet in the opposite hand.

As the words carried on the breeze, the gentleman's mission became apparent. He was reading his original poetry with verve and passion. Having sketched his soul onto paper, he was driven to read aloud so anyone, everyone, could hear what stirred the cauldron of his heart.

Whether or not anyone listened seemed inconsequential to this gifted artist. The important thing was that his creation had to find a way to express itself.

Suddenly, the visionary moved toward people strolling in the park and sitting comfortably on benches. "Five cents," he announced boldly. "Just a nickel for a copy of my poetry."

Some onlookers shrugged their shoulders and turned their backs as they walked away. Others reached into pockets and fumbled for change. Elderly women searched for coins in their over-stuffed purses.

The passion in his eyes was evident. He loved what he was doing. First, marshaling his feelings into words. Second, delivering those words with a commanding presence. Third, making that financial transaction. People were paying for poetry that cried out of his pounding chest and mind.

Some people love sports. Others love music. Others love cars. Some children love animals. Blessed is the person who has meaning and purpose, who can hardly wait to get out of bed in the morning.

Another Ten Things I Love
Sharing With You

open-air concerts

newly mown lawns

the fragrance of lilacs

a hearty laugh

more chocolate

a thank-you note

a neighbor's wave

bread pudding

an inspiring sermon

the final car payment

Part Seven:

True Love Is Consistent

"My food," said Jesus, "is to do the will of him who sent me and to finish his work. Do you not say, 'Four months more and then the harvest'? I tell you, open your eyes and look at the fields! They are ripe for harvest."

JOHN 4:34-35

How Does Your Garden Grow?

God Almighty first planted a garden. And indeed, it is the purest of human pleasures.

FRANCIS BACON

Early in the spring, Don planted a garden behind his house where it could get plenty of sunshine. Every morning from the kitchen window he and his wife watched how the garden was growing.

Radishes and peas broke through the soft soil first. Tulips began to bloom along the borders. The colors, the blossoms, the daily changes brought newness and excitement.

As the weeks came and went the couple enjoyed their garden's produce. Planting, watering, growing, harvesting, each in its turn, each had its place. Each season was in its own way better than the one before.

Strawberries, cucumbers, tomatoes, string beans, cantaloupes, pumpkins—they came forth in their time. The garden grew and added to their enjoyment each day, each week and every month.

One September day Don stood by the kitchen window. As he looked out into the backyard he thought, "A garden is like our love. Each season has its own pleasure to give. At first it seems so exciting when the plants come up. But as the plants grow, the next season is even better than the previous one."

Gardens take planning. They take time. Healthy gardens require water. Weeds come up from time to time. A few bugs get in and do damage if the garden isn't watched. But a garden that is cared for and tended creates happiness season after season.

Healthy love is never planted and then abandoned to care for itself. It, too, must be watered and watched over to bring forth the greatest joy. And if it is, each season of love grows and becomes better and better.

Lover, how does your garden grow?

Love Is ...

Love is very patient and kind,
never jealous or envious,
never boastful or proud,
never haughty or selfish or rude.

Love does not demand its own way.
It is not irritable or touchy.
It does not hold grudges and
will hardly even notice when others do it wrong.
It is never glad about injustice,
but rejoices whenever truth wins out.

If you love someone you will be loyal to him
no matter what the cost.
You will
always believe in him
always expect the best of him, and
always stand your ground in defending him.

1 CORINTHIANS 13:4-7 TLB, emphasis added

I Love You Enough to Show Up

Love begins when a person feels another person's needs to be as important as his own.

HARRY S. SULLIVAN

A famous movie star was asked the key to good acting. With considerable modesty he replied, "Showing up."

Early on in his marriage Mark learned a similar lesson about caring. When he was first married, he loved his wife tremendously. If they were apart for any length of time, he thought about her constantly. His heart ached because he missed her so much. And yet, despite deep feelings for the woman he loved, he had one glaring fault. Mark repeatedly failed to show up.

When Mark's wife wanted boxes moved to the basement, her husband was busy golfing. When she needed to talk about her problems at work, Mark was watching a ballgame. During the terrible days of morning sickness, Mark went to the office an hour early.

Not that Mark didn't care. He really did. Unfortunately, he just didn't realize that part of caring for someone is being there for him or her. And so, time after time Mark simply failed to show up.

One day, frustrated and overloaded, Emma let him know exactly how she felt. "Let's face it," she said. "When I need you the most, you're never here."

"Why, of course I am," Mark protested.

But he knew the accusation was true. For years he had cared *about* Emma, but seldom was there to care *for* her. And because he really did love her, from that day on, slowly but surely, things began to change.

That's not to say that he doesn't sometimes make mistakes. Emma is learning to use those times to reach out to others for help and encouragement. But every time he's there to load the car, their marriage becomes a little stronger. Each time he holds Emma and listens to the things that most concern her, that investment pays rich dividends.

He may never win the "Most Outstanding Husband" award, but that really isn't important. The fact is that he now knows a great deal more about showing up.

Love doesn't just lay there,

like a stone,

it has to be made,

like bread;

re-made all the time,

made new.

URSULA K. LEGUIN

A Daily Passion

Firm and steadfast in good works make me,
and in Thy service make me to persevere.

CLARE OF ASSISI

Mari Sandoz had a driving passion for writing. Her book *Old Jules* is about her pioneering father who broke the sod of western Nebraska. When asked how she managed to become a published author, Mari gave this formula.

She would get a job, almost any job, and earn fifty dollars. Immediately the spirited dreamer would quit that job and begin to write for long, dedicated days. When the money exhausted itself, she would search for another job. After collecting another fifty dollars, Mari would again tender her resignation.

Writing was her daily passion. Her love for the craft and the basic need to express herself on paper marched only half a step behind her needs for food, housing and sleep.

Not all love is directed toward people or God. Some of the deepest and most obvious love is found in meaning and purpose.

Listen to a child describe his love for a pet. Hear

the woman who waxes eloquent about the day-care center for at-risk children that she operates. Consider the person who is drawn to climb a mountain simply "because it's there."

These people are not talking about casual hobbies or flickering interests. Their passion for a particular task becomes a burning fire inside that will not be quenched.

We can't be sure if people with deep passions actually live longer, but they seem happier. They have reason to get up in the morning. They have a goal to accomplish and a sense of victories won. They have discovered the joy of a job well done.

Happy is the person who steps back and says to himself, "I loved it; I loved doing it; and I would love to do it again."

Let It Be Me!

O daughters of Jerusalem, I charge you —
if you find my lover,
what will you tell him?
Tell him I am faint with love.

Song of Songs 5:8

Would you like to be with someone you can trust implicitly? Someone who will not lie or deceive you? Someone who is open enough to prize the truth and promise to deliver it day after day? I want to be that person.

Let it be me!

Would you like to find someone who will share his most intimate feelings with you? Love and hope as well as hurt and fear? Do you want to find someone who is caring enough to listen to your feelings, too? Will you be patient while he reaches inside his heart and shows you how he feels? I want to be that person.

Let it be me!

Do you want to find a person who will be strong? Not movie-star strong, but real live, dependable strong? The kind of person who will not walk away? The kind of person who stands beside you when things get tough and disappointments rise up and surround you? Do you want someone who will not become flaky, who will not cut and run? I want to be that person.

Let it be me!

How would you like to find someone who understands integrity and commitment? A true partner who will not shop around? A partner who does not keep his options open? Someone who is a one-person lover? Is faithfulness that important to you? Then I know whom you should choose …

Let it be me!

Maybe you'd appreciate a partner who likes to go out once in a while. Dinner, a movie, a walk in the park. An evening now and then, just to make you feel special. I'd like to be that person for you. And if sometimes I guess wrong about the things you might enjoy, will you be grateful that I tried?

Let it be me!

Could you be happy with someone who took the time to say "I love you"? Not a quick, meaningless expression but the direct, slow, sincere kind. The kind that starts deep inside and rolls out warmly. If that is what you want for the rest of your life, then the choice is clear ...

Let it be me!

Love Is Like a Flashlight

All things come to him who waits,
provided he knows what he is waiting for.

WOODROW WILSON

Anita couldn't find a flashlight. Doggedly she opened drawers all over the house. Diligently she checked under chair cushions and riffled through stacks of newspapers. To no avail she searched behind doors and opened cabinets.

Finally out of frustration she looked deep behind a dark staircase. In order to see better Anita turned on the flashlight that she was holding in her own hand.

This is a true story.

Sometimes our restless hunt for love makes us forget that we already have it. The most important love we will ever know is the love we hold in our own control.

Our great gift is the love we are able to give, not the love we hope to get.

A pity beyond all telling
Is hid in the heart of love.

W.B. YEATS

The Gift of Love
Is for Everyone

And now these three remain:
faith, hope, and love.
But the greatest of these is love.

1 CORINTHIANS 13:13

When God made us in his image, he could have passed along any number of God-like qualities to us.

He could have given us the ability to know everything. If he had, we could cure cancer and the common cold. We would have been able to pass every exam in school simply by showing up and filling in the correct boxes.

On the other hand, God might have shared his unique gift of being everywhere at once. We could have walked through quiet gardens in Bombay and sailed the Pacific Ocean—at the same time. A gift like that would have eliminated carpools and answering machines.

But God did not choose to pass these gifts on to us. Perhaps he thought it would have muddled up our lives too much. Instead he gave us something better.... He instilled in each person the amazing ability to love. Each time we take a risk and decide to love, we do something that is God-like.

The very act of love allows us to step outside ourselves and touch the heart of another human being. With love we touch our spouse, our friends, our relatives and the child down the street.

Only God could build majestic canyons or hang stars in space. None of us can begin to measure up to such astounding feats. But the simple, sincere act of caring for someone else is one miracle that we are all capable of performing.

Home is a place not only of strong affections, but of entire unreserve; it is life's undress rehearsal, its backroom, its dressing room, from which we go forth..., leaving behind us much debris of cast-off and everyday clothing.

HARRIET BEECHER STOWE

Going Home?

But Ruth replied, "Don't urge me to leave you or to turn back from you. Where you go I will go, and where you stay I will stay. Your people will be my people, and your God my God. Where you die I will die, and there I will be buried. May the Lord deal with me, be it ever so severely, if anything but death separates you and me."

RUTH 1:16-17

Our first year of marriage ran like an old lawn mower. Some days it ran smoothly. Other days it wouldn't start. Sometimes our relationship sat motionless, going nowhere.

This happens to most lovers at some time, but we didn't know that then.

I was in graduate school. We were broke and far from family. Our efficiency apartment was one room and a bath. Life seemed overloaded with responsibility.

One evening, when life felt dull, I simply blurted out my frustration. "Pat," I began fearfully, "do you ever think about going home?"

Immediately she turned and gave me "that" look.

Every husband knows what "that" look means. Indeed everyone who had a mother knows "that" look.

Pat gave me her look and said without emotion, "Bill, I am home."

Stunned, I knew the discussion was over. She removed all uncertainty and eliminated any debate. Pat wasn't going anywhere. This left me with no choice but to work things out. Her response said our marriage was here to stay.

I thank God for a stubborn wife. If she had equivocated, argued or left a crack in the door I would have rushed in. Who knows what dumb thing I might have said? Our relationship could have been damaged beyond repair.

Sometimes love is at its best when it digs its heels in and holds tight.

Love is, above all, the gift of oneself.
                                        JEAN ANOUILH